THE WIZARD OZ

Choral Revue

Arranged by GREG GILPIN
Orchestrated by PETE SCHMUTTE

Alfred Music
P.O. Box 10003
Van Nuys, CA 91410-0003
alfred.com

ISBN-10: 0-7692-7055-7
ISBN-13: 978-0-7692-7055-5

THE WIZARD OF OZ
Choral Revue
SATB, accompanied

Arranged by
GREG GILPIN (ASCAP)

Approximate performance time: 10:05

Grandioso, ♩ = 72

MUNCHKINLAND
Music by HAROLD ARLEN,
Lyric by E.Y. HARBURG*

CM97119

fell from a star. She brings you good

fell from a star. Oo

news or have -- n't you heard? When she

fell out of Kan - sas a mir - a - cle oc --

6

kitch - en took a slitch, it land - ed on the wick - ed witch in the

pitch. It took a slitch.

mid - dle of a ditch. Which _____ was not a health - y sit -

- u - a - tion for a wick - ed witch who _____ be - gan to

DING-DONG! THE WITCH IS DEAD
Music by HAROLD ARLEN, Lyric by E.Y. HARBURG*

Lyrics:

Ding - Dong, the witch is dead! Which old witch? The wick - ed witch.

Ding - Dong, the wick - ed witch is dead! Ah _____

Wake up, you sleep - y head, rub your eyes, get out of bed.

12

Ding - Dong! the mer - ry - o sing it high, sing it low.

Let them know the wick - ed witch is

dead!

LULLABY LEAGUE/
LOLLYPOP GUILD
Music by HAROLD ARLEN,
Lyric by E.Y. HARBURG*
optional trio

CM97119

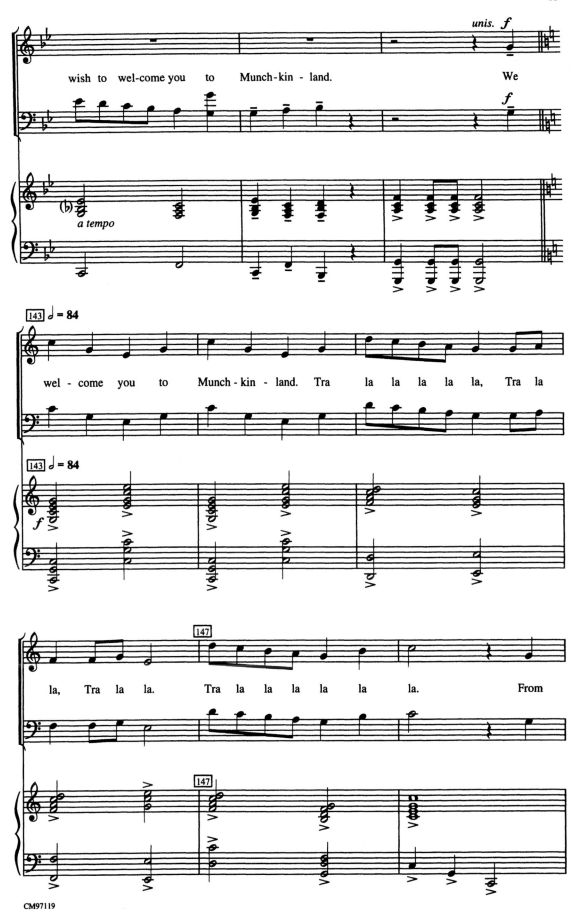

WE'RE OFF TO SEE THE WIZARD
Music by HAROLD ARLEN,
Lyric by E.Y. HARBURG*

won - der - ful Wiz - ard of Oz. _____ We hear he is a

whiz of a wiz if ev - er a wiz there was. If

ev - er, oh ev - er a wiz there was, the Wiz-ard of Oz is one be - coz, be -

20

IF I ONLY HAD A BRAIN
Music by HAROLD ARLEN, Lyric by E.Y. HARBURG*

friends with the spar-rows and the boy that shoots the ar - rows, if I on - ly had a heart. ____

(Lion) Solo 3 *mf*

____ Oh, I'd ____ be in my stride, a

king down to the core, oh, I'd roar the way I nev - er roared be -

fore, and then I'd rrwoof, and roar some more. I would

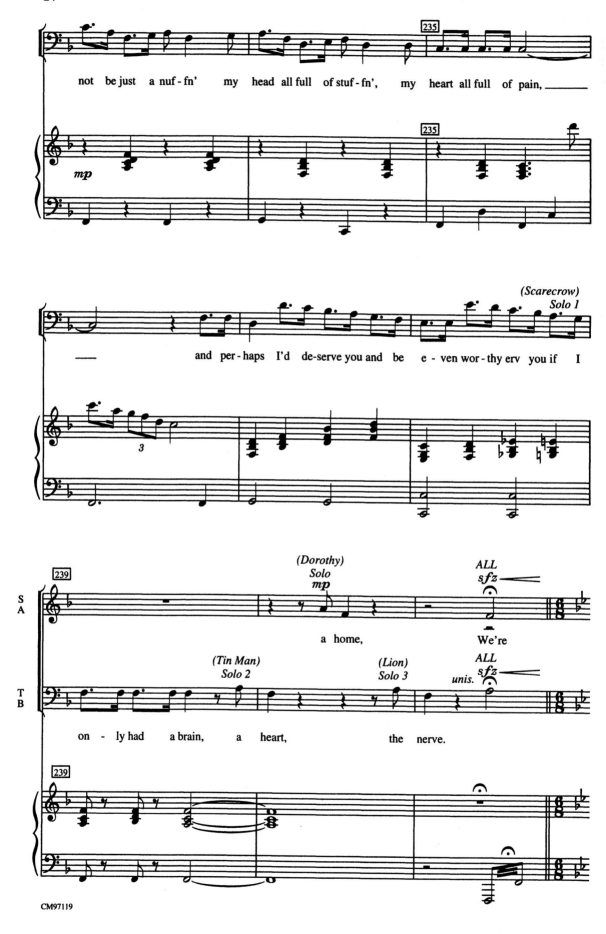

not be just a nuf-fn' my head all full of stuf-fn', my heart all full of pain, _____

(Scarecrow) Solo 1
_____ and per-haps I'd de-serve you and be e - ven wor-thy erv you if I

S A

(Dorothy) Solo mp
a home, We're

(Tin Man) Solo 2 _(Lion)_ Solo 3 unis.
ALL sfz
T B
on - ly had a brain, a heart, the nerve.

Miss Gulch's Theme
(with Lions and Tigers and Bears and March of the Winkies)

Li-ons and ti-gers and bears, oh, my!   Li-ons and ti-gers and bears, oh, my!

Li-ons and ti-gers and bears, oh, my!

Li-ons and ti-gers and bears, oh, my!

O - ee - oh,   Yoh

O - ee - oh,   Yoh

Ah

OPTIMISTIC VOICES
Music by HAROLD ARLEN and HERBERT STOTHART,
Lyric by E.Y. HARBURG*

CM97119

place on the face of the earth or the sky.

Hold on - to your breath, hold on - to your heart, hold on - to your hope.

March up to that gate and bid it o - pen, o - pen!

div.

unis.

L'Istesso tempo *rit.* *mp*

THE MERRY OLD LAND OF OZ
Music by HAROLD ARLEN, Lyric by E.Y. HARBURG*

mer-ry old land of Oz. "Bzz-'bzz-'bzz, chirp, chirp, chirp, and a

cou-ple of la - de - das." That's how the crick-ets crick all day in the

div. legato
mp

mer-ry old land of Oz. We get up at twelve and start to work at

350 OVER THE RAINBOW

(Dorothy)   Music by HAROLD ARLEN, Lyric by E.Y. HARBURG*

CM97119